NATIONAL GEOGRAPHIC

D0503620

Plants in the Park

Dimi Stanos

Plants grow in the park.

This plant grows in the park.

This plant grows in the park.

This plant grows in the park.

This plant grows in the park.

This plant grows in the park.